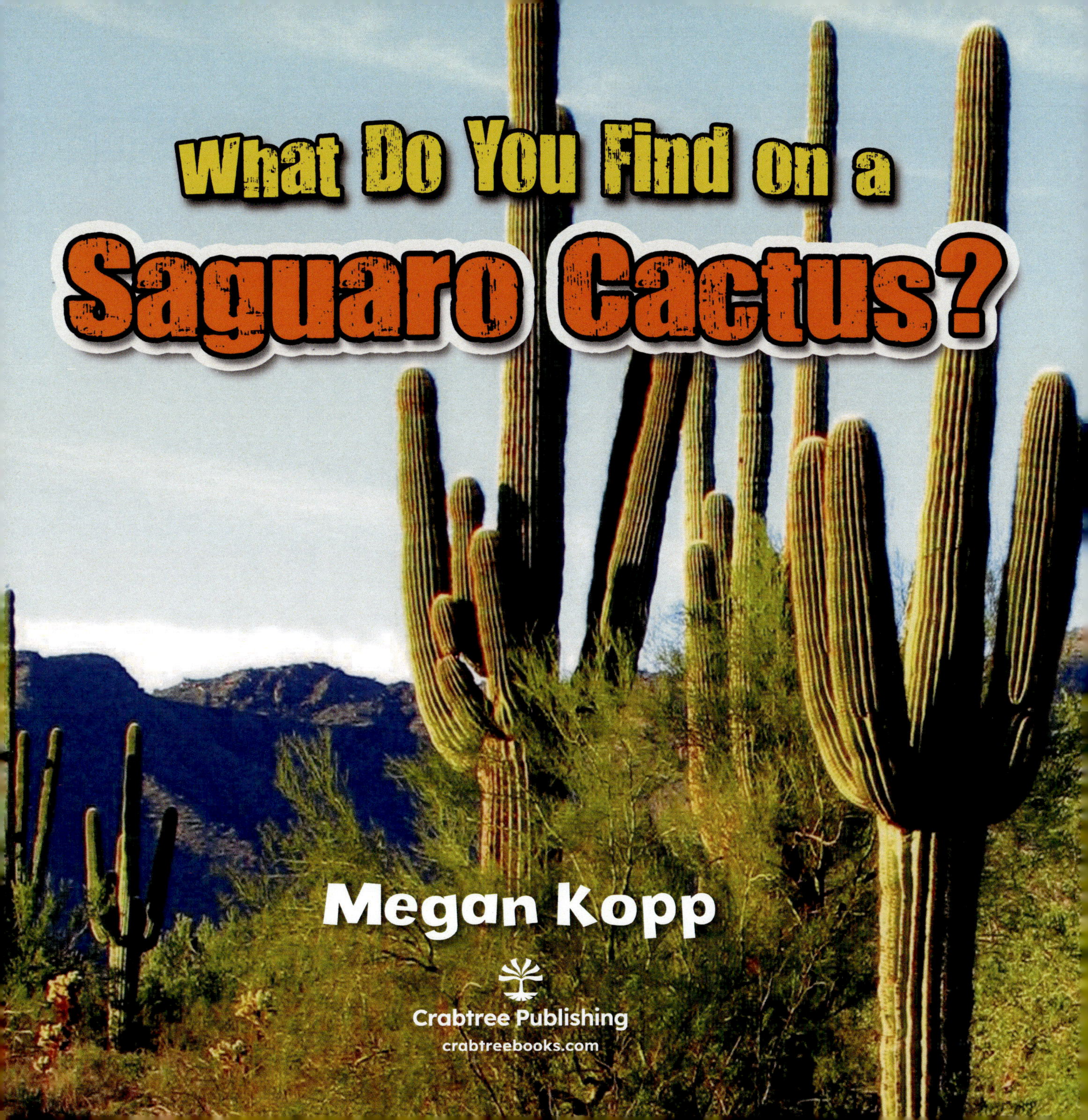

What Do You Find on a Saguaro Cactus?

Megan Kopp

Crabtree Publishing
crabtreebooks.com

Ecosystems Close-Up

Crabtree Publishing

crabtreebooks.com 800-387-7650

In Canada: We acknowledge the financial support of the Government of Canada through the Canada Book Fund for our publishing activities.

Author: Megan Kopp
Publishing plan research and development: Reagan Miller
Editors: Janine Deschenes, Crystal Sikkens
Design: Ken Wright, Tammy McGarr (cover)
Photo research: Janine Deschenes, Crystal Sikkens
Production and prepress: Ken Wright
Print coordinator: Katherine Kantor

Library and Archives Canada Cataloguing in Publication

Kopp, Megan, author
What do you find on a saguaro cactus? / Megan Kopp.
(Ecosystems close-up)
Includes index.
Issued in print and electronic formats.
ISBN 978-0-7787-2265-6 (bound).--
ISBN 978-0-7787-2289-2 (paperback).--
ISBN 978-1-4271-1727-4 (html)
1. Desert animals--Juvenile literature. 2. Saguaro--Juvenile literature.
3. Saguaro--Ecology--Juvenile literature. 4. Desert biology--Juvenile literature. 5. Desert ecology--Juvenile literature. I. Title.
QH541.5.D4K67 2016 j591.754 C2015-907996-9
C2015-907997-7

Published in Canada
Crabtree Publishing
616 Welland Avenue
St. Catharines, Ontario
L2M 5V6

Published in the United States
Crabtree Publishing
347 Fifth Avenue
Suite 1402-145
New York, NY 10016

Illustrations:
Barbara Bedell: page 22 (jackrabbit)

Photographs:
iStockphoto: pages 15 (cactus fruit), 18, 19
Thinkstock: pages 12 (cactus), 16, 20 (cactus model)
Wikimedia Commons: Rennett Stowe: page 1; Maximilian Dorrbecker: page 4 (inset); Federal Government of the United States: page 15 (kangaroo rat)
All other images from Shutterstock

Hardcover 978-0-7787-2265-6
Paperback 978-0-7787-2289-2
Ebook (pdf) 978-1-4271-1727-4

Printed in Canada/112024/CP20241128

Library of Congress Cataloging-in-Publication Data

Names: Kopp, Megan, author.
Title: What do you find on a saguaro cactus? / Megan Kopp.
Description: New York, NY : Crabtree Publishing Company, [2016] | Series: Ecosystems close-up |
Identifiers: LCCN 2016001305 (print) | LCCN 2016002059 (ebook) | ISBN 9780778722656 (reinforced library binding : alk. paper) | ISBN 9780778722892 (pbk. : alk. paper) | ISBN 9781427117274 (electronic HTML)
Subjects: LCSH: Saguaro--Juvenile literature. | Saguaro--Ecology--Juvenile literature. | Desert ecology--Juvenile literature.
Classification: LCC QK495.C11 K67 2016 (print) | LCC QK495.C11 (ebook) | DDC 583.56--dc23
LC record available at http://lccn.loc.gov/2016001305

Contents

What is a Desert?

Deserts are dry areas with very little rainfall. Deserts are normally very hot during the day and cold at night. Even though they can be hard places to live, many plants and animals find special ways to stay alive.

*The **Sonoran Desert** is a desert found in the southwest part of North America.*

These saguaro cacti in Arizona can live in very hot temperatures.

Living in a Desert

Many animals come out only at night when the Sun goes down. This is when it is cool enough to move around. Desert plants, such as cacti, save water. The saguaro cactus is the largest cactus in the United States. It lives only in the Sonoran Desert.

The Saguaro Cactus Ecosystem

A system is made up of pieces working together. Each part of the system relies on each other. An **ecosystem** is a system made up of all the living and nonliving things found in one place. A saguaro cactus is a type of ecosystem.

Sand, sunlight, and air are some of the nonliving things found around a saguaro cactus ecosystem.

What do you Think?

Looking at this **model**, can you identify which things are living and which are nonliving?

We can use models, such as this computer diagram of a saguaro cactus ecosystem, to help us understand how things are connected.

A Working System

Plants and animals are living things. Living things change as they grow. They make new living things. Plants grow seeds to start new plants. Animals have babies. Nonliving things are not alive. They cannot grow or change.

Life in the Desert

Living things need both nonliving and other living things to **survive** in the desert. Air, sand, water, and sunshine are all nonliving things. We do not always notice nonliving things, but they are important parts of life in the desert.

Saguaro cacti can live over 200 years and grow up to 60 feet (18 m) tall.

Needs to Meet

Plants need water, air, and sunlight to make their own food. This food gives them **energy** to grow. Animals need air, food, water, and **shelter** to stay alive. Plants and animals only live in ecosystems where their needs are met.

What do you Think?

How does the saguaro cactus depend on nonliving things?

Desert Air

All living things need air to survive. Air is a nonliving thing. It is found all around the saguaro cactus ecosystem. Insects take in air through holes along the sides of their bodies. Animals, such as foxes, breathe air with their lungs.

Desert birds, such as this greater roadrunner, breathe air with lungs.

Cool Ears

Desert air is hot and dry during the day. Desert foxes have extra large ears. When desert breezes blow over the foxes' ears, the warm blood in their ears is cooled. The cooler blood flows back through the fox's body. This helps them stay cool.

A jackrabbit's large ears release heat from their body. This helps them stay cool in the desert.

Drink it up!

All living things depend on water to survive. In the Sonoran Desert it is hot and dry for most of the year. Plants that live here, such as the saguaro cactus, grow very slowly because there is not a lot of water.

The saguaro cactus has tiny spines instead of leaves. The spines don't need much water.

A Thirsty Cactus

A saguaro cactus can survive up to two years without rain. Its roots spread out far across the ground. This helps the cactus take up water from the ground quickly. Water is stored in the cactus's stem and branches. Plants and animals depend on the saguaro cactus for water.

Desert bighorn sheep eat pieces of saguaro cacti when there is no water to drink.

What do you Think?

Trees with a lot of big leaves need a lot of water to survive. Would trees with big leaves grow well in a desert ecosystem?

Finding Food

Living things need food in order to live and grow. Plants make their own food using sunlight, air, and water. Animals cannot make their own food, so they get energy from eating other living things.

Desert tortoises eat plants such as grass and wildflowers.

Eating in the Desert

Some animals eat only plants. The seeds inside saguaro cactus fruit are a good source of energy. Kangaroo rats eat seeds, and also spread seeds for new saguaro cacti as they move around. Some animals eat other animals. Tiny elf owls hunt small animals like kangaroo rats.

What do you Think?

What would happen to this food chain if kangaroo rats were taken from the ecosystem?

*A **food chain** shows how energy moves from one living thing to another in an ecosystem. This is an example of a saguaro cactus food chain.*

Home Sweet Cactus

Many animals use a saguaro cactus for shelter. They can hide there from animals that want to eat them, or use it to escape the heat in its cool, dark inside. Some animals also use a saguaro cactus to raise their babies.

Some large birds make nests between the arms of saguaro cacti.

This gila woodpecker looks out from its saguaro cactus home.

Birds of a Feather

Saguaro cacti are big enough that some animals can live inside them. Woodpeckers make a cactus home by pecking holes in the trunk to lay eggs. Other birds, such as owls, will then use these holes to stay safe from other animals, or keep cool from the Sun.

What do you Think?

Imagine there were no more saguaro cacti in the Sonoran Desert. What would happen to these desert birds?

Protecting the Saguaro Cactus

Saguaro cacti are often used for yard decorations in the American southwest. They are expensive to buy. Some people take them from the wild and then sell them for use in gardens.

It is important to treat the saguaro cactus ecosystem with respect. Many living things depend on it to survive in the desert!

Saguaro cacti help decorate this garden in California.

Doing More Harm Than Good

Taking a wild saguaro cactus out of its environment is against the law. It harms the natural desert environment and affects many kinds of animals.

A Model Home!

Scientists use models to help us understand how things are connected. A model is a **representation** of a real object. A model can show how different parts of something work together. Maps, pictures, storyboards, and diagrams are kinds of models.

Show how living and nonliving things are connected in a saguaro cactus ecosystem by creating your own model.

Materials you will need:

- modeling clay
- a pencil
- construction paper
- scissors
(make sure an adult is present)
- information in this book

Create your Model

Your own model of a saguaro cactus ecosystem should show how living things meet their needs. Remember that living things need food, air, water, and shelter to survive.

Follow these steps to make your own clay cactus model:

1. Use your pencil, construction paper, and scissors to draw and cut out plants, animals, and nonliving things that you can find in a saguaro cactus ecosystem.
2. Use modeling clay and build a saguaro cactus.
3. Stick the plants and animals on or around your cactus. Put the living things in the shelters where they would live. Make sure they have the food, water, and shelter they need to survive.

Dig a Little Deeper

Scientists use models to help them learn more about the systems they study. Now it is your turn!

- Choose one of the living things in your model.
- Tell family and friends what might happen if it disappeared from the ecosystem. Which other living things would be affected? Why?

Sharing knowledge helps us learn! Explain how each part of an ecosystem has an important role to play.

Learning More

Books

Fredericks, Anthony D. *Around One Cactus*. Dawn Publications. 2003.

Orizotti, Andy Garreffa. *Good Morning Sonoran Desert.* Lulu Publishing Services. 2014.

Profiri, Charline. *Guess Who's in the Desert.* Rio Chico. 2013.

Rabe, Tish. *Why Oh Why Are Deserts Dry?: All About Deserts.* Random House Books for Young Readers. 2011.

Websites

Arizona-Sonoran Desert Museum: Saguaro Cactus Fact Sheet
www.desertmuseum.org/kids/oz/long-fact-sheets/Saguaro%20 Cactus.php

National Park Service: Saguaro Cactus in Oregon Pipe Cactus National Monument.
www.nps.gov/orpi/learn/nature/saguaro-cactus.htm

Science Kids: Fun Cactus Facts for Kids
www.sciencekids.co.nz/sciencefacts/plants/cactus.html

Words to know

ecosystem [EE-koh-sis-tuhm] (noun) all the living things in a place and their relation to the environment

energy [EN-ur-jee] (noun) the ability to do things

food chain [food cheyn] (noun) the order of living things in an ecosystem by which food energy is passed from one to another

model [MOD-l] (noun) a representation of a real object

representation [rep-ri-zen-TEY-shuhn] (noun) a picture, drawing, model, or other copy of something

shelter [SHEL-ter] (noun) the place where living things are safe

Sonoran Desert [suh-NAWR-uhn DEZ-ert] (noun) a desert found in the southwestern United States and northwestern Mexico

survive [ser-VAHYV] (verb) to stay alive

A noun is a person, place, or thing. A verb is an action word that tells you what someone or something does.

Index